WEATHER AND CLIMATE

WEATHER WATCH

FORECASTING THE WEATHER

by Ellen Labrecque

CAPSTONE PRESS
a capstone imprint

Capstone Captivate is published by Capstone Press, an imprint of Capstone.
1710 Roe Crest Drive, North Mankato, Minnesota, 56003.
www.capstonepub.com

Library of Congress Cataloging-in-Publication Data is available on the Library of
Congress website.
ISBN: 978-1-5435-9156-9 (library binding)
ISBN: 978-1-4966-5778-7 (paperback)
ISBN: 978-1-5435-9161-3 (ebook pdf)

Summary: Describes how meteorologists use different tools to predict weather,
including severe weather.

Image Credits
Alamy: dmac, 23, National Geographic Image Collection, 17, Ryan McGinnis, 7,
ZUMA Press, Inc, 24; Newscom: Gary W. Green/MCT, 16, PATRICK SCHNEIDER,
4; North Wind Picture Archives, 10; Science Source: David R. Frazier Photolibrary,
Inc, 21, Science Stock Photography, 29, U.S. Army, 14; Shutterstock: aapsky, 15, 18,
19, BONNIE WATTON, 25, Cire notrevo, 5, Dan Ross, 6, djgis, cover, 1, FloridaStock,
27, fotografermen, 12, FotoKina, 8, FrameStockFootages, 28, leonrwoods, 11
(bottom), Morphart Creation, 13, pedrosala, 22, ssuaphotos, 9, Trong Nguyen, 26,
txking, 11 (bottom)

Artistic elements: Shutterstock: ArtMari, Creative Stall, gigi rosa, MaddyZ, Rebellion
Works, rudall30

Editorial Credits
Erika L. Shores, editor; Tracy McCabe, designer; Kelly Garvin, media researcher;
Kathy McColley, premedia specialist

Words in **bold** are in the glossary.

All internet sites appearing in back matter were available and accurate when this
book was sent to press.

Capstone thanks Laura M. Klein, M.S., Ph.D., for her expertise in reviewing
this book.

Printed and bound in the USA.
PA99

TABLE OF CONTENTS

CHAPTER 1

WILD WEATHER

Roads were packed with cars. People were told to leave. Weather reports said a **hurricane** was soon going to slam into the coast. Huge wind gusts would wreck houses. High ocean waves would flood streets. As much as 30 inches (76 centimeters) of rain would fall. If people stayed, they would become trapped. But people knew the storm was coming. They could leave the area and get to safety.

When a hurricane is expected, people living along coasts need to move inland to be safe.

Usually we know when bad weather is coming. Millions of lives are saved every year. How is it done? Let's learn how people **forecast**, or predict, the weather.

Extreme winds from hurricanes push water onto land where it floods streets.

FLYING INTO THE STORM

Special airplanes fly into hurricanes. They do this to find out wind speeds and other information. These airplanes can hold up in very strong winds. Pilots say it feels like being on a wicked roller coaster ride.

Weather is one of the most powerful forces on Earth. Lightning storms start fires. **Tornadoes** tear up towns. **Monsoons** cause flooding and mudslides. We need to know when bad weather is coming. We can get ready and be safe.

Tornadoes move quickly along the ground.

The study of weather is called **meteorology**. Meteorology looks at the daily changes that take place in our **atmosphere**. It can be hot and sunny one minute. It can be raining the next. Meteorologists are the people who predict these changes.

To make a forecast, a meteorologist studies weather maps showing current conditions.

Climatology is the study of weather over a longer period of time. Climatologists predict changes in weather patterns for months and years. Humans are causing **climate** change. This is a change in our weather over a long period of time.

Activities such as cutting down trees and driving cars that burn gasoline are bad for the earth. They put **carbon dioxide** into the air. With too much carbon dioxide in the air, climate changes. Storms form more often. They also are stronger. Floods and **droughts** are more likely than in the past. Because of climate change, our weather is becoming more extreme. This makes forecasting the weather more important than ever.

Climate change is causing hurricanes to be longer and stronger.

All the carbon dioxide from cars is a big cause of climate change.

FACT

Ice at the poles is melting because of climate change. In turn, melting ice causes oceans to rise. Oceans are expected to rise between 1 and 6 feet (0.3 and 1.8 meters) by 2100.

CHAPTER 2

WEATHER FORECASTING OVER THE YEARS

Long ago, people tried to tell what the weather would be like based on **observations**. They studied nature. They watched for signs. They wrote down what they saw. The information they gathered helped them tell if it was going to rain. It told them which way the wind was blowing. They also watched the moon, stars, and sun. This helped them plan their days. They could decide when it was safe to travel. They could decide when it was best to plant crops.

Farmers prepared for cold weather. They put grass and dirt around their homes to make them warmer.

Tools helped people better predict the weather. The barometer was invented in 1643. A barometer measures air pressure. When air pressure drops, clouds and wind often arrive. This means a storm might be coming. The thermometer we use today was invented in 1714. A thermometer measures the air **temperature**.

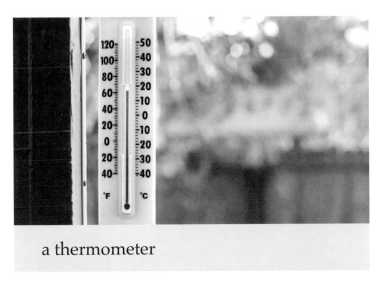

a thermometer

a barometer

About 150 years ago, the telegraph made it possible to share weather forecasts around the world. A telegraph was a machine that sent and received messages. Ship captain Robert FitzRoy knew many sailors died in storms at sea. He started a warning service for ships. FitzRoy received telegraph messages of warnings about storms. He then sent these messages to sailors at other spots. The messages warned them about what was coming their way.

a telegraph

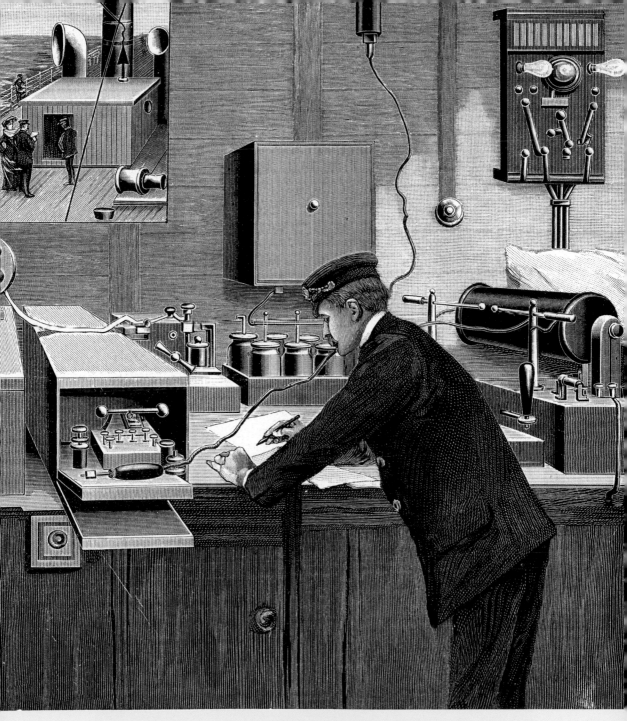

Ships that received telegraph messages about storms could change their routes to avoid bad weather.

The next big change in forecasting came with weather **satellites**. These objects in space take pictures of the weather on Earth. They send the information back to Earth. With these pictures, scientists can predict what the weather will be like days before it happens.

TIROS-1 was the first weather satellite put into use. It was sent into space about 60 years ago. This satellite snapped photos of moving clouds as it traveled between the North and South Poles. It floated about 400 miles (640 kilometers) above Earth.

TIROS-1 was the first weather satellite.

Over the years weather satellites have gotten better. Today satellite pictures of clouds help track rainfall, snow, ice, wind speeds, and more.

A satellite over a hurricane in the Atlantic Ocean

FACT

Weather satellites can even tell how hot or cold parts of the ocean are. Fish like warm water. People who fish use this weather data to decide when and where to fish.

CHAPTER 3

WEATHER FORECASTING TODAY

The NOAA (National Oceanic and Atmospheric Administration) tracks weather in the United States. NOAA's giant computers receive weather information from space, the air, and the oceans. Together, it all helps predict the weather. When you see a weather forecast on TV or online, these findings started with NOAA's research. One part of NOAA is called the National Weather Service (NWS). NWS workers make weather, water, and climate forecasts as well as send out weather warnings for the United States.

NOAA's computers fill a huge room.

NOAA has weather offices in every state in the country.

SATELLITES

NWS uses two types of weather satellites to predict the weather. One is called a polar orbiting satellite. It circles Earth close to the North and South Poles. It flies over the same spot twice a day. It is about 530 miles (860 km) up in space. It helps weather scientists make daily forecasts.

A satellite in polar orbit

The other is called a geostationary satellite. This type is as high up as 22,000 miles (35,400 km). It orbits Earth at the same speed as Earth rotates. This means it can hang over one area of our planet. By staying in one spot, it is able to tell when big storms form.

A satellite orbiting Earth

WEATHER BALLOONS

Twice a day, NWS workers release 92 weather balloons all over the United States. These balloons provide information to help scientists forecast. The information collected also helps scientists study climate change.

A transmitter, called a **radiosonde**, is tied to each balloon. The radiosonde sends facts, like wind speed and direction, to equipment on the ground. As the balloon rises, it bursts due to air pressure. A parachute on the radiosonde helps it slowly fall to the ground. It then can be picked up and used again.

FACT

Each radiosonde has a mailing bag that tells you what to do if you find one. You should return it. It will be used again.

A meteorologist is set to release a weather balloon.

DOPPLER RADAR

NWS also uses **radar**. The Doppler radar system sends out radio waves from a giant antenna. When these radio waves strike something in the air, like rain, it sends these waves back. The radio waves that return are changed in shape and position. There is also a change in the number of waves that come back each second. From the information sent back, scientists can see where rain, hail, or snow is. They can also predict where the storm is headed.

A giant white dome covers the Doppler radar antenna.

Radar systems can even spot some tornadoes. The radio wave hits random swirling shapes like leaves and grass high in the air. This means a tornado may be forming or may already be on the ground.

Computer maps show the information from a Doppler radar.

CHAPTER 4

SEVERE WEATHER

Weather scientists use the same tools to predict severe weather as they do everyday weather. But it is harder to predict bad weather. It usually occurs in a smaller area than regular weather conditions. It doesn't last a long time.

A meteorologist looks at weather maps to keep track of storms.

Meteorologists can't predict severe weather far into the future. Storms form quickly. Sometimes they only spot a tornado minutes before it hits. Flash flooding can happen when a thunderstorm brings heavy rainfall. The rain falls too fast and has no place to go. Rivers overflow. The rushing water can cause huge mudslides with no warning.

Flash flooding caused by heavy rainfall can wash away cars and roads.

Weather forecasters do everything they can to help people stay safe in bad weather. They put out severe weather warnings. They use colors to tell the danger level and what kind of storm is coming. For example, a hurricane warning is red.

Sometimes it is hard to decide whether to tell people to leave an area. Storms change their paths often. If people leave and no storm comes, money and time are wasted. But if they don't tell people to leave and the storm hits, lives can be lost. That is much worse.

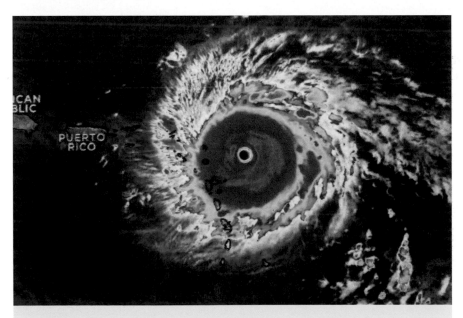

The bright red on this weather map shows a giant hurricane.

Red flags at a beach warn people swimming is not allowed because the weather is too dangerous.

HURRICANE SEASON

People who study hurricanes can predict how many might form during the season. In the Atlantic Ocean, the season lasts from June 1 to November 30. During that time, 12 tropical storms may form. Half of them might become hurricanes.

THE FUTURE OF WEATHER PREDICTION

Weather is tricky. A storm can pop up that wasn't forecasted. Another one can miss an area when all forecasts said it would hit. Today a five-day forecast is right 90 percent of the time. A 10-day forecast is only right half the time.

Meteorologists track a hurricane.

New and better weather tools are always being put in use. Some of these might help scientists predict weather farther into the future. Meteorologists are getting closer to having daily and weekly forecasts be right more often than ever before.

A meteorologist uses information from all kinds of weather tools in order to predict the weather.

GLOSSARY

atmosphere (AT-muhss-fihr)—the mixture of gases that surrounds Earth

carbon dioxide (KAHR-buhn dy-AHK-syd)—a gas that is produced when people and animals breathe out or when certain fuels are burned and that is used by plants for energy

climate (KLY-muht)—the average weather in a place over many years

drought (DROUT)—a long period of weather with little or no rainfall

forecast (FOR-kast)—to predict future changes in weather conditions; a forecast is a report of what the weather may be in the future

hurricane (HUR-uh-kane)—a strong, swirling wind and rainstorm that starts on the ocean; hurricanes are also called typhoons or cyclones

meteorology (mee-tee-ur-AWL-uh-jee)—the study of weather

monsoon (mon-SOON)—a very strong seasonal wind that brings heavy rains or hot, dry weather

observation (ob-zur-VAY-shuhn)—a habit of watching and noticing

radar (RAY-dar)—a weather tool that sends out radio waves to figure out the size, strength, and movement of storms

radiosonde (REY-dee-oh-sond)—an instrument attached to a weather balloon that records weather related items like temperature and wind speed

satellite (SAT-uh-lite)—a machine that is sent into space and that moves around Earth

temperature (TEM-pur-uh-chur)—the measure of how hot or cold something is

tornado (tor-NAY-doh)—a spinning column of air that looks like a funnel

READ MORE

Hayes, Amy. *Meteorology and Forecasting the Weather.* New York: PowerKids Press, 2019.

McAuliffe, Bill. *Forecasting.* Mankato, MN: Creative Education, 2018.

Schwartz, Heather E. *Tracking a Storm.* Huntington Beach, CA: Teacher Created Materials, 2019.

INTERNET SITES

The National Weather Service for Kids
https://www.weather.gov/cae/justforkids.html

Predict the Weather
https://kids.nationalgeographic.com/explore/nature/predict-the-weather/

Weather Observations
https://www.noaa.gov/education/resource-collections/weather-atmosphere-education-resources/weather-observations

INDEX